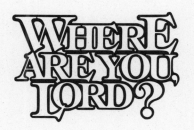

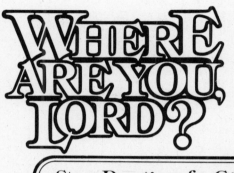

WHERE ARE YOU, LORD?

Story Devotions for Girls

MARY ANN KERL

AUGSBURG Publishing House • Minneapolis

WHERE ARE YOU, LORD?

Copyright © 1982 Augsburg Publishing House

Library of Congress Catalog Card No. 82-70949

International Standard Book No. 0-8066-1924-4

Scripture quotations marked RSV are from the Revised Standard Version of the Bible, copyright 1946, 1952, and 1971 by the Division of Christian Education of the National Council of Churches.

Scripture quotations marked TEV are from the Good News Bible, Today's English Version: Copyright © American Bible Society 1966, 1971, 1976. Used by permission.

Illustrations by Tom Maakestad.

MANUFACTURED IN THE UNITED STATES OF AMERICA

*To the nieces
the good Lord blessed me with—
Shirley, Michelle, and Lisa*

Contents

About This Book

Where are you, Lord?

That's the question I asked when I was a girl. Some days I thought the Lord was busy with grown-ups and had forgotten me. But I was always delighted to discover differently. Even so, I remember thinking that when I grew up I would have it made. Then I thought I would never have to ask, "Where are you, Lord?" anymore.

Now I *am* grown up. I have two sons. But you know what? I still ask, "Where are you, Lord?" As a matter of fact, I asked that question more than ever as I wrote this book.

You see, my 10-year-old son's good friend, Rachel Curtis, was going to help me write this book. Rachel was my friend too. I thought she was great. How excited I was when she told me she would help. What fun we'll have writing this book together! I thought.

Imagine how sad I was when Rachel was killed in a bicycle accident. "Where are you, Lord?" I asked when I sat at Rachel's funeral. "Where are you, Lord?" I said when Rachel's brother came to visit us—alone. "Where are you, Lord?" I questioned when I saw Rachel's mother—without Rachel. *"Where are you, Lord?"* I demanded when I saw my son playing —by himself.

After I asked that question a million times, a most wonderful thing happened to me. I am not so sad anymore. As a matter of fact, I get excited and happy when I remember Rachel is in heaven now. I can just see her big brown eyes, black hair, and that wide smile across her face as she holds the Lord's hand. I can just see Rachel skip with the Lord on those gold-paved streets. Rachel Curtis has it made! She never has to ask, "Where are you, Lord?" anymore!

The Lime Green
Notebook Paper

"Pssst. Can I borrow a sheet of paper?" Susan whispered to Marcia.

Marcia swung her long red hair back from her face and gasped. "But you owe me three sheets already!" she whispered from her school desk.

Susan said she knew that. Actually Susan did not know that—not exactly. She was new at Brentford School, and she assumed when you borrowed paper it would be the same as it was at Redbud Middle School. Redbud was the school Susan attended before she moved. At Redbud, everyone borrowed everything and no one reminded anyone to pay anything back. The children there figured with everyone borrowing, things would come out even at the end of the school year anyway.

Susan wished she were back at Redbud. Redbud was a small school. She had lots of friends there.

Brentford was a large school. Susan had no friends here.

"Just be patient," Susan's mom had told her. "We've only been here three weeks. You'll find friends."

Ha! Susan laughed to herself. *How can I make friends when no one notices me?* she wondered.

"Time to get your notebook paper and pencils out for history class," Mrs. Ryley, the sixth-grade teacher, said.

Susan leaned forward in her desk. "Well, can I have a sheet of paper, Marcia? Please?"

Marcia flipped her royal blue notebook open, displaying several paper tablets. "Tell you what," Marcia said, "pay me back my three sheets first, and then you can borrow one."

"But if I had three sheets of paper, I wouldn't need one now," Susan whispered.

Marcia put her hand on her chin and whispered loudly. "Hmmmm. The new girl is smart in math," she said, smirking. The boys and girls sitting nearby giggled. Susan hung her head.

"I said get ready for history class, everyone," Mrs. Ryley said in a firm voice. "Susan, that means you, too. Get some paper from your desk please."

Susan fumbled nervously in her desk. Of course, Susan did not have any paper to get. For three days she had forgotten to tell her mother she needed notebook paper for school, but she didn't think that would be a problem. She was out of paper for two weeks once at Redbud and had all the paper handouts she wanted.

When Mrs. Ryley went to the blackboard, Susan quickly whispered to several of the boys and girls to ask if she could borrow some paper. One of the boys,

Ted, folded his arms, propped a red pencil behind his ear, and said, "No, I'm most sorry, but you can't have any paper. Your credit, I understand, isn't too good."

The class started laughing. Susan hung her head. Mrs. Ryley tapped the edge of a ruler on her desk.

"Class! Class!" she ordered. "Settle down."

When Mrs. Ryley started writing on the blackboard, Susan leaned further toward Marcia's desk. "May I borrow another sheet?" she whispered. "Please?"

Marcia frowned and slowly got another sheet from her notebook. "Oh, I guess," she said, handing Susan the paper. "But don't forget to pay me back. Tomorrow."

Tomorrow! Of all the nerve, Susan thought. She felt her cheeks get hot. No one at Redbud would have said that. She put one hand to the side of her mouth and whispered, "Forget I ever borrowed it! I'll never ask you for paper again, and I won't pay you back either!"

Marcia's blue eyes stared at Susan. "I won't forget it," Marcia said.

Mrs. Ryley put the chalk she was holding on the chalkboard. "Susan and Marcia, come to the front of the room," she commanded.

Marcia scampered to her feet. "You're in trouble now," she whispered to Susan as she headed for the front.

Susan got up slowly from her seat. Her heart pounded. Never had she been called to the front of the room at Redbud. *Why had she talked that way to Marcia?* she wondered. For being a Christian, she really messed things up some days. This, apparently, was one of those days.

"Now," Mrs. Ryley began when the two girls got to the blackboard, "what's the problem?"

"Mrs. Ryley," Marcia blurted, "Susan said she's not going to pay back the four sheets of paper I let her borrow from me."

Mrs. Ryley raised her eyebrows and peered over her glasses at Susan. "Is that true?" she asked.

Susan hung her head and shrugged her shoulders. "Well . . ." she hesitated.

"Just a yes or no will do," Mrs. Ryley stated.

"Yes," Susan mumbled. But before she could explain how things like this operated at Redbud, Mrs. Ryley told Susan to take her seat for a moment while she talked with Marcia.

"Then I'll talk with you," she added, instructing the class to study the history lesson for a few moments while she took care of this matter.

The longer Marcia and Mrs. Ryley talked, the harder Susan's heart pounded. Every now and then Marcia would nod her head and say something in a low voice. Mrs. Ryley said a bunch of things in a low voice. Then she told Marcia to sit down and asked Susan to come forward.

"Now, why did you tell Marcia you weren't going to give her the paper you borrowed?" Mrs. Ryley asked in a quiet voice.

Susan shrugged her shoulders.

"But you must have had a reason for telling Marcia that. What was it?" Mrs. Ryley insisted.

"Well, at the school I came from . . ." Susan stammered.

14

Mrs. Ryley leaned forward. "Yes, what about the school you came from?" she asked.

"Well, when we borrowed paper there we never paid it back," Susan said.

"Never?" Mrs. Ryley asked, raising her eyebrows again.

"Well, usually never. We just figured it'd come out even in the end anyway rather than keep track of it."

Mrs. Ryley folded her arms, frowned, and said, "Hmmmm. I see. Probably it did come out even in the end. That's fine. As long as everyone remained friends, I see nothing wrong with that. But did Marcia know that?" Susan hung her head. Mrs. Ryley placed her hand on Susan's shoulder. "You see, no one here does it that way. We can't. This school is too large for that. We have classes in different rooms, not in just one room like you did at Redbud. I'm afraid if we did it the way you did at Redbud, everyone would get all mixed up, and things wouldn't turn out even in the end at all."

Mrs. Ryley smiled at Susan. "Would you really want Marcia to borrow paper from you and not pay you back ever?"

Susan scraped one scuffed shoe on top of another. "No, I suppose not," Susan said.

"Sometimes it's hard to move," Mrs. Ryley added, still smiling. "Often things aren't done the same as they were done at the place we've moved from. But you must accept the change, Susan. Now, you need to pay Marcia back as soon as you can. OK?"

Susan nodded. But that was going to be hard. She dreaded giving Marcia the paper back. She could just imagine it. Marcia, probably sneering, would grab the paper, tear it into shreds, toss it over her shoulder, and say, "Confetti anyone?" Or maybe Marcia would make paper airplanes for everyone out of it to show off. Or worse yet, Marcia would probably take the paper and say, "It's about time you paid me back." Then she would go with the rest of the class and ignore Susan.

The next day at school, Susan walked to Marcia's desk. Her heart was pounding again as she handed Marcia four sheets of a bright-colored lime green notebook paper. "Here," she said quietly.

"Hey, neat!" Marcia said, smiling as she took the paper. "Where'd you find this color? I get so sick of white!"

"At Harper's Department Store," Susan answered.

"Do they have any more like it?" Marcia wanted to know.

"I don't know. But I'll trade you some, if you like," Susan added.

"Oooh. Would you trade 10 sheets?"

"Sure," Susan answered, pulling 10 sheets from her notebook.

"Thanks!" Marcia exclaimed. "Hey, you want to come shopping with me Saturday to see if I can buy a whole notebook of this just like yours? I'll ask my mom if she'll take us."

"Sure," Susan smiled as the morning class bell rang. *Maybe*, she thought, *Brentford School won't be so bad after all.*

> He who withholds kindness from a friend forsakes the fear of the Almighty.
>
> Job 6:14 RSV

Oh, Lord, sometimes I forget things I borrow and do not pay my friends back. Forgive me when I say I do not owe them. Oh, Lord, help me to remember to be kind.

A Card for Mr. Phillips

At the nursing home, Julie filed in line with the rest of her Sunday school class. They had come to visit the elderly people and give them the greeting cards they had made in Sunday school the previous week. Now Julie was wishing she had not come. Everywhere she looked she saw old people that reminded her of her grandfather.

It was hard for Julie to imagine her grandfather dead. She remembered all the times he gave her quarters for Eskimo Pies and butterscotch candies when she was little. She remembered how she went to his house one day when she lost her rag doll and was too scared to go home. *How will I ever manage without Granddad?* she wondered.

After the funeral, things got worse for Julie instead of better. "Time will help you," her mom and dad had told her. "We all miss Granddad, but he's happy in heaven now and he died without pain. He didn't even have to go to a hospital. It's better this way."

But Julie did not believe it was better this way. She would rather have visited her grandfather in a hospital than put flowers on his grave. Julie missed him more than ever. Every day that passed was worse than the day before. Soon she began thinking about all sorts of horrible things.

Is Granddad's body decaying now? she wondered. *Does Granddad know what's going on, or is death like sleeping? How will I die? When will I die? Will it hurt?*

Julie had never thought much about death before, but she had never known anyone that died before either. Julie did not want to die—ever! She wished she could be like Elijah or Enoch. *How nice it would be,* she thought, *just to scoot up to heaven without dying first.* But Julie also knew that was not likely to happen. She had not heard of anyone doing that lately.

"I'm sure the people here will love the cards you made for them," Mrs. Ambers, her Sunday school teacher, was saying. She instructed the class to go to the rooms and hand out the cards. "Then after that we'll sing some hymns for the people here in the lobby."

Julie started giving her cards to several ladies in the lobby. One was in a wheelchair. "Thank you," each of the ladies said. "How lovely."

"You're welcome," Julie said politely. Then she trotted down the hallway and went into a room at the end of the hall.

"Wait! Don't go in there!" a nurse, racing down the hall, called to Julie. But it was too late. Julie did

not hear the nurse and skipped into the room. She came to a halt when she saw the old man in the bed. He was completely still, except for his eyelids that fluttered now and then. As he lay there, curled in a knot with his knees almost touching his chest, he groaned softly. Drops of perspiration were on the old man's temples where his purple veins puffed underneath the skin. His cheeks were sunken in and masses of wrinkles covered his face. The old man looked strangely familiar to Julie.

"He won't need a card," the nurse said softly to Julie. "Come, you can go into the next room."

The old man blinked his eyes open. "Card? What card?" he grunted.

"Nothing, Mr. Phillips, just go ahead and rest," the nurse said cheerfully as she patted the man's shoulder. "Come, let's go," she said to Julie, taking her hand.

Mr. Phillips frowned at Julie. "I don't want your stupid card. It's nothing but junk," he snorted. "Get outta here! Leave me be!"

"Sure, Mr. Phillips, we'll let you rest," the nurse said, still with a cheerful tone. "Have a nap, and I'll bring you a nice supper. How does that sound?"

"Just don't bring me lime Jello!" Mr. Phillips snapped.

"No lime Jello?" the nurse chuckled. "No, I won't bring you any if you don't like it. Tell you what though. I'll bring you something special. How about some chocolate cake for dessert?"

The man closed his eyes again. "Dunno, maybe," was all he said as he drifted back to sleep.

Tears were in Julie's eyes when she went into the hall with the nurse.

"He really doesn't think your card is junk," the nurse said to Julie.

"Why did he say it then?" Julie asked.

"We have to give Mr. Phillips so much medicine that sometimes he doesn't know what he's saying."

"How come?"

The nurse took a handkerchief from her pocket and wiped Julie's tears. "Because Mr. Phillips is in a lot of pain," the nurse answered. "He hurts very much. He's dying. We want to make him as comfortable as we can until God takes him to heaven."

"Will he go there today?" Julie wanted to know.

The nurse shook her head. "Only God knows the answer to that," she said. "He could, but he also could be here for a long time yet. He's been with us five years now."

"Five years?" Julie asked.

"That's right," the nurse nodded, smiling, "and I'm afraid those years haven't been easy for Mr. Phillips. He's been sick with cancer all those years and has suffered a lot."

Julie told the nurse that her grandfather went to heaven only a few weeks ago.

"He did?" the nurse asked. "Did he live with us? Maybe I knew him."

Julie told the nurse no. "He lived in a house of his own," she said. "I went there a lot."

"He died suddenly then?" the nurse asked.

Julie nodded her head. "The doctor said it was a heart attack," she said.

"He was very lucky," the nurse said.

Julie frowned. "He was lucky to have a heart attack?" she asked.

"I know it doesn't sound right," the nurse answered, "but what I mean is, it takes some people, like Mr. Phillips, a long time to die."

Julie twisted the handkerchief the nurse had given her. "But—but Granddad was nice," she said. "He'd never have talked to you like Mr. Phillips did."

The nurse smiled. "Before Mr. Phillips had to take medicine, he was nice too."

"He was?"

"He was indeed. How well I remember when he first came here. Would you believe he picked a rose from our flowerbeds every day for me?"

"He did?"

"Yes," the nurse said, "and he did a lot more than that too. He used to give sacks of candy and fruit to the children every year at Christmas, and at Easter Mr. Phillips dyed dozens of eggs. He just had a generous and cheerful heart." Tears were now forming in the nurse's eyes.

Julie gasped. "*That* Mr. Phillips!" Julie exclaimed. "I know him! I remember the sacks of candy and Easter eggs. He was a friend of my grandfather's."

The nurse smiled. "You don't say!" she exclaimed.

Julie asked if she could go back to Mr. Phillips's room. In the room, the nurse fluffed Mr. Phillips's pillow. "We've just discovered this young lady is a friend of yours," the nurse said, bending over Mr. Phillips.

The old man blinked his eyes open and grunted.

"Don't you remember me?" Julie asked. "My grandfather was Ted Williams."

Mr. Phillips leaned forward on one arm. "Ted Williams," he said, a smile spreading across his face. "Well, glory be! You've grown up a tad since I last seen you, my girl."

24

Julie shrugged her shoulders. "A little," she said. "Remember the purple eggs you made for me?"

"Ha, do I remember?" Mr. Phillips chuckled. "One year I gave you red ones by mistake, and you returned them all the next day. Oh, those were the days!"

In the distance, Julie heard her class singing. "Oh, dear," she said, "it's time to sing already."

"Singing today, are ya? Sing real loud and maybe I can hear you," Mr. Phillips said.

"OK. I'll come back and visit another day too, if you'd like," Julie said.

Mr. Phillips smiled, showing his false teeth that appeared a little too large for his mouth. "I'd like," he said.

"OK. Good-bye, Mr. Phillips. I'll tell Mom and Dad I saw you too."

"You do that."

Julie started to skip out of the room. "Wait a minute, young lady!" Mr. Phillips snapped. "Haven't you forgotten something?"

Julie stopped. "What?" she asked.

"My card," Mr. Phillips said, smiling.

> If the Spirit of him who raised Jesus from the dead dwells in you, he who raised Christ Jesus from the dead will give life to your mortal bodies also through his Spirit which dwells in you.
> Romans 8:11 RSV

Thank you, Lord, for dying on the cross so we can someday go to heaven. Help me remember this when someone I love dies.

The Van Kids

When the bell rang for math class, Patty got up from her desk to go to the van.

"Hey, why does she have math in the van, anyway?" Mark whispered to Jerry. "Why can't she stay here with the rest of us?"

"I don't know," Jerry said, staring at Patty. He raised his forefinger to his head and spun it in circles. "Maybe it's because she's crazy! Maybe all the van kids are crazy!"

Patty felt awful. *Why do I have to go to the van?* Patty wondered. She knew it was because she had a learning disability, whatever that was. She even liked going to the van. There were fun things there. The van had special calculators and computers. But Patty did not like her classmates to see her go to the van. Every day she had to get up from her desk and leave for math and English classes. How the other kids

stared at her! How Patty hated it! And now this—
Jerry saying maybe she was crazy . . . .

At home, Mrs. Stewart asked Patty how school was.
"Fine, of course!" Patty snapped. "Why do you always
have to ask anyway?" But she did not wait for her
mother to answer. Instead she raced up the stairs,
flopped on her bed, and sobbed. She felt a horrible
sick feeling, like a big lump, in her stomach.

Is Jerry right? Am I crazy? Patty wondered. *Is that
what a learning disability means?* Tears streamed
down her oval-shaped face.

"Oh, Lord," Patty prayed, "why did you give me a
learning disability anyway? Did I do something bad?
Is that why I'm not like the other kids?"

When Patty heard footsteps, she dried her tears
with her hands. She did not want her mom to know
she had been crying. But Mrs. Stewart could tell, and
she asked what was the matter. "Why are you upset,
Patty? Can you tell me?"

"Can't," Patty started sobbing again. She buried
her head back in the pillow. Mrs. Stewart put her
hand on Patty's back.

"Tell God then," Mrs. Stewart said.

"Already did. He wasn't listening," Patty mumbled.

"I'll bet you he was," Mrs. Stewart said, smiling.
"Have you given the Lord a chance to answer? Sometimes it takes him longer than we like to answer our
prayers. But I'm sure he heard you, Patty, and he will
help."

Patty was not so sure. When she got up the next
morning, the lump in her stomach felt even worse.
She had to tell someone, some grown-up person. That
was the only way to get rid of a stomach lump. But
Patty could not tell her mom, much as she loved her.

If I am crazy, Patty thought, *I sure don't want Mom to know it. Maybe I could ask my van teacher. I do like Mrs. Matthews, and she's supposed to know how to help kids like me.*

In the van, Patty planned to tell Mrs. Matthews her problem without crying. But when she got to the big question, Patty could not help it. Tears streamed down her freckled cheeks. Her chin trembled. "Is what Jerry said true?" Patty whispered, her voice shaky. "Am I crazy?"

Mrs. Matthews reached across her desk for a yellow tissue. She handed the tissue to Patty and told her that indeed she was not crazy.

Patty blew her nose. "But what can I do when someone calls me that?" Patty wanted to know.

Mrs. Matthews tapped her red pencil on the desk. "Hmmmm," she said, wrinkling her forehead. "I may have an idea." Then Mrs. Matthews stretched back in her chair, put her hands behind her head, and smiled. "Patty," she began, "how would you like to teach math in your regular classroom today?"

"Math?" Patty gasped. Math, as Mrs. Matthews knew, was Patty's best and favorite subject. Patty clasped her hands together. "Could I really?"

Mrs. Matthews said she would arrange it with Patty's regular classroom teacher, Mrs. Dixon.

"But how would that help me?" Patty wanted to know.

The class bell rang. Mrs. Matthews leaned forward in her chair and took Patty's hand. "I'm sorry I don't have time to explain it," Mrs. Matthews said, smiling. "You need to get to your next class. But you'll find out in math class. I think this idea just may work. Trust me."

Later that afternoon, when the bell rang for math, Mark turned in his desk. "Hey," he whispered to Patty, "didn't you hear the bell? You'd better get to the van."

But Patty said she was not going there for math today.

"How come?" Mark wanted to know.

Just then Mrs. Dixon announced she had a surprise for math class. She walked to the door and nodded her head. "Please come in, Mrs. Matthews," Mrs. Dixon said.

Mrs. Matthews walked to the front of the room. "Your teacher tells me you're having a little trouble with fractions," Mrs. Matthews said. The class groaned, all except Patty. Mrs. Matthews brushed her short, dark hair back from her forehead with her hand. "I thought you'd like some help. Patty, will you please come to the front of the room and begin today's lesson?" Mrs. Matthews asked.

Patty went to the front of the room and told the class to open their math books. "Fractions are super simple," Patty began.

"Huh? Are you crazy?" Mark blurted. "I hate fractions."

"Yeah, Patty, you've got to be kidding," Sally, another classmate, said. "Fractions are super hard!"

"She's not kidding! She's crazy!" Jerry announced.

Mark jerked his hand in the air. "Yeah, I'll vote on that," he said. "Everyone that thinks fractions are hard and Patty is crazy, raise your hand!"

The hands that went up did not ease the lump in Patty's stomach. Mrs. Dixon clapped her hands. "Class! Class!" she ordered. "Settle down. Now, who

has some questions on fractions for Patty? She's here to help you."

Mark jumped up, slammed his hands on his hips, and said, "If you think fractions are so simple, tell me, what's one-fourth plus one-third?"

Patty crossed her arms and tapped a finger on her chin. "Ahhh—that's seven-twelfths."

"Seven-twelfths?" Mark shouted. "Never heard of it!"

"But it's the correct answer," Mrs. Dixon stated. She walked to Patty and handed her some chalk. "Here, show Mark how you got your answer."

Patty wrote three times four equals twelve on the board. Mark folded his arms and shrugged his shoulders. "Three times four equals twelve," he read out loud, sighing. "I already know that."

"But did you know it's the common denominator for your problem?" Patty asked.

"Common what?" Mark frowned. The class giggled.

Patty wrote more figures on the board, explaining them as she went. "Since one-third is equal to four-twelfths," Patty explained, "and one-fourth is equal to three-twelfths, all you have to do is add the three plus the four and put them over twelve, your common denominator, for the right answer."

Mark scratched his head. "Where were you last night when I was struggling through this stuff?" he asked. The class giggled again.

Patty smiled as more hands rose. Nearly everyone had a question for Patty on fractions. Patty felt good as she answered the questions, one at a time. For each question, Patty wrote the complete problem and answer on the board.

Just before math class was over, Mark raised his hand again. But this time he did not have a question about the lesson. "How come you're such a genius with fractions anyway?" he asked Patty. "I thought the van kids didn't know math very well."

"Or anything else!" Ted added.

"Yeah," several others joined in.

Mrs. Matthews went to the front of the room and stood beside Patty. "The children that go to the van, like Patty, are learning disabled," she began to explain.

"What does that mean?" Mark interrupted.

Mrs. Matthews thought for a few seconds, then went to her purse and pulled out a small card. "Look," she said, holding up the card. "This is my driver's license. On it there's an X marked in the square labeled glasses. Now, does that mean I can't drive a car?"

"I hope not!" Jerry gasped. "You gave me a ride in the red van one morning."

"Me too," several others joined in.

"That's right, I did," Mrs. Matthews nodded, taking off her black-framed glasses. She held the glasses high for everyone to see. "And don't worry. I can drive *if* I'm wearing my glasses. You see, I have a disability with my eyes. Without my glasses, I couldn't drive. I wouldn't see the road signs and other important things."

Mrs. Matthews put her glasses back on and continued. "But with my glasses, I see just fine. My eyes just need special help, that's all. That's the way it is with Patty. Just because she has a learning disability doesn't mean she can't learn. It just means Patty needs special help, help that I can give her in the van, with our special equipment. She's doing eighth grade math, by the way."

"But we're only in the sixth grade," Jerry exclaimed.

"That's exactly why Patty goes to the van for math. She's way ahead and is working faster in math than everyone here," Mrs. Dixon explained. From the ooh's and ah's, the class apparently was impressed.

Mark raised his hand again. "I don't have a learning disability, and I'm in the sixth grade, right?" he asked.

"That's right," Mrs. Dixon and Mrs. Matthews agreed.

Mark sighed and flung his arms in the air. "Then how come I can't do sixth grade fractions?"

Once again the class giggled.

"Everyone's good in some things and poor in others, whether he or she has a learning disability or not," Mrs. Matthews explained, smiling. "But when someone has a learning disability, he or she is often extra-good in some subjects and extra-poor in others."

"What's Patty extra-poor in?" Mark wanted to know.

"English," Patty groaned. "I hate it. I'm only doing fourth grade English."

Sally jumped up. "I love English," she said. "Looks like you and I could be good friends. Since I'm ahead of you in English, I could teach you that, and since you're ahead of me in math, you could teach me fractions."

Mrs. Dixon and Mrs. Matthews both agreed this was a good idea. "Now class, before we end our math hour, how would you like Patty to come again soon to help us with math?" Mrs. Dixon asked.

Mark jumped up, stuck out his chest, cupped his

hands around his mouth, and shouted "Bravo! Bravo!" Jerry joined him. The rest of the class jumped up, clapping their hands. Patty grinned. The lump in her stomach was gone.

> Whoever thinks he knows something really doesn't know as he ought to know.
>
> 1 Corinthians 8:2 TEV

Oh, Lord, forgive me when I call someone crazy when I am trying to act smart. Forgive me when I act like I know all the answers. Teach me to love.

Magic Tricks for the Banquet

"What are you wearing tonight?" Joan asked Helen.

Helen pretended she did not know what Joan meant. "Wearing? Tonight?" Helen asked, blinking her blue eyes.

"You know," Joan said, "for the Daughter-Dad Banquet."

Helen smoothed her long blonde hair from her face with her hands. "Oh, that," Helen said casually. "I decided not to go."

"But everyone's going!" Joan said, gasping.

Helen shrugged her shoulders and kicked some gravel. "Aw, that stupid banquet's getting boring."

Joan stared at Helen. "Eating spaghetti and hot fudge sundaes with a bunch of skits and funny songs afterwards is boring? Besides, you and your father always entertain us with your magic tricks."

Helen put a bounce to her walk and a smirk on her face. "Oh, you know how it is," she said. "We decided to wait for Hollywood to call us. Nothing but big time shows for us from now on."

"I bet I know what you're up to," Joan went on to say, not paying attention to Helen's remark. "You and your Dad are planning to surprise us, like you did last year. That's it, isn't it? You're going to surprise us as part of your magic act, aren't you? Come on, Helen, I'm your best friend. You can tell me. I promise not to tell anyone."

Helen remembered the fun she had with her father and the magic tricks. Last year they did a disappearing act. Helen's father had put a sheet over Helen while she squeezed into a box the people could not see. Then when her father pulled the sheet and shouted "Presto!" there was no one in the original box. Helen remembered giggling in the other box. The audience had gone crazy.

"I just bet that's it," Joan said again. "You're going to do just what you did last year. The announcer's going to say there won't be magic tricks this year, and then bang! right in the middle of the show, the lights will blink three times and you and your dad will run on stage. That's it, isn't it?"

Helen wished that was it. *Why did he have to leave anyway?* Helen wondered. *It's not fair! His leaving spoils everything! We'll never do our magic tricks again!*

Ever since her father had gone, Helen had felt a sick growl in her stomach. She wondered if 12-year-olds ever got ulcers.

"Well, is that it or not?" Joan asked.

Helen thrust her hands into the pockets of her

navy blue coat and walked faster. "Will you be quiet about that stupid banquet?" Helen said. "I wouldn't go to that dumb banquet if I was the last person on earth."

Joan started walking as fast as Helen. "But why not?" Joan asked.

"'Cause I don't have a father!" Helen blurted. She did not want to tell Joan that, but lately she seemed to be saying a lot of things she did not want to say.

"Of course you have a father," Joan said.

"Do not!" Helen cried.

"Helen, you're not making any sense. Everyone knows your father."

"Will you stop it?" Helen screamed, running ahead of Joan. "My father doesn't live at our house."

Joan ran up to Helen. "Well, why not?" she insisted. "Where did he go? Why did he leave? I saw him there last week."

Last week was ages ago. Doesn't Joan realize that? Helen wondered. *Last week everything was fine. But this week—wow! Could things ever change in a week!* It was only Tuesday when Helen found out about the divorce. A big, thick envelope had come in the mail. When Helen handed it to her mom and asked if it was important, her mom just opened it and cried.

Why hadn't Mom told me before? Helen wondered. *Why hadn't she said things weren't going right?* Oh, sure, she knew her parents would not get any awards for being happy. She remembered the fights—sometimes at night she heard them fighting when they thought she was asleep, but in the morning, at the breakfast table, everything seemed all right again, as though nothing happened the night before. Helen did notice her dad did not kiss her mom when he came home from work anymore. *But that's no big deal*, Helen thought. *So what? Maybe they just decided to do their kissing when no one was looking.* At least that was what she hoped. But then her dad just moved out . . . .

"Why doesn't your dad live at your house anymore?" Joan was asking.

"None of your business!" Helen snapped, running up the driveway to her home, leaving Joan bewildered.

When Helen walked in the house, she spotted the letter. It was addressed to her. No return address, but that did not matter. Helen recognized the handwriting. It was the second letter her father had sent this week. Helen did the same thing with this letter she did with the first. Without opening it, she tore it into shreds. Then she pushed the torn shreds to the bottom of the wastebasket.

That evening, while they were at the supper table, the telephone rang. "If it's him, I'm not here," Helen told her mom.

Whenever Helen's father called, Helen refused to talk to him. She knew this silent treatment upset her mother, but Helen could not help it. *There's no way I'm going to talk to him after he deserted us,* Helen kept thinking. *What did I ever do wrong? It's not fair! It's not my fault they got a—a divorce.* That word always stuck in her throat, even if she did not say it out loud.

"Honey, I do wish you'd talk to your father," her mother said, walking to the phone. "Are you sure you won't change your mind? Can't you be nice to him? He's not angry at you. Why are you angry at him?"

Helen remained silent.

"Hello," Mrs. Williams said. "Yes, Helen's here, but I'm afraid she still doesn't want to talk . . . umhumm . . . yes, that would be fine."

Even if Helen did not want to talk to her father, she sure wished she could hear what he was saying. *Probably just trying to cause more trouble*, she thought.

After the supper dishes were done, Helen's mother told her to put on her pretty pink dress and good shoes.

"But why? I'm not going anywhere," Helen said.

"Your father is coming here tonight, and I want you to look nice," Mrs. Williams answered.

Helen threw down the dish towel. "Mother, how could you?" she cried.

Helen wanted to look as bad as she felt, but Mrs. Williams made her take a bubble bath, brush her teeth, and put on the pink dress.

"You do look nice," Mrs. Williams exclaimed after Helen was dressed.

"Don't feel nice," Helen muttered.

Mrs. Williams took Helen's hand and sat beside her on the sofa. "I know this isn't easy for you, honey," she said, "but try to remember it hasn't been easy for any of us. I don't want you to be angry at your father."

The doorbell interrupted Mrs. Williams. "There. I bet that's your father now," she said as she gave Helen's thick hair a last-minute brush job.

"What's all the big fuss?" Helen asked.

Mrs. Williams kissed Helen on the forehead and went to the door. "Hi, John," she said.

John nodded. "How are you?" he asked.

Helen thought the whole thing was crazy. Her parents were talking as though they were strangers.

"Is my date ready?" Helen's father asked, his blue eyes sparkling. He raised his dark blonde eyebrows when he saw Helen. "Hey, looks like you're all set," he said, clasping his hands together and smiling.

Helen stared at her father. He was wearing a black suit, white shirt, and dark red tie. He never wore clothes like that unless he was going somewhere important. He walked towards Helen, bent down, and gave her a kiss on the cheek. Helen hated to admit it, but wow! his spice after-shave lotion smelled as good as it always did.

"Now, young lady," her father said, "are you ready for some magic tricks?"

"Magic tricks?" Helen asked.

"You haven't forgotten?" Mr. Williams asked. "We are going to the banquet, aren't we?"

"I didn't know you remembered when it was," Helen said.

"How could I forget?" Mr. Williams asked. "It's the first weekend every May. That's why I sent the letters. I didn't want you to forget."

"I didn't forget. I thought you'd forget," Helen said.

Mr. Williams nodded his head and sat on the sofa beside Helen. "I think I'm beginning to understand," he said. "You think because I divorced your mother I'm going to divorce you too."

Helen hung her head and gave her shoulders a shrug. "Something like that," she mumbled.

Mr. Williams squeezed Helen's hand. "There's no way I'd divorce you," he said.

"There isn't?" Helen asked.

"There isn't," Mr. Williams answered. "I love you too much."

Mrs. Williams knelt in front of Helen and her father. "That's why we made sure your father got visitation rights when we got our divorce."

"Visitation what?" Helen asked.

"That means your mother was kind enough to allow me to come and see you every weekend," Mr. Williams explained.

"Every weekend?" Helen asked.

"That's right," Helen's father said.

"But that's more than I saw you when you lived here," Helen said.

Mr. Williams looked off into space for a moment and then said, "Yeah, I know. Maybe that's one of the reasons your mother and I couldn't get along anymore." Then he looked at his watch. "Anyway, for right now, we'd better hurry. We wouldn't want to be late, would we?"

"But I already told Joan I wasn't going," Helen said.

Mr. Williams raised his eyebrows and smiled. "Well, won't she be surprised!" he exclaimed.

Helen jumped from the sofa and raced upstairs to her bedroom.

"Helen, Helen, please," her mother called. "Come back down here. Where are you going?"

In no time at all, Helen bounced down the stairs carrying a small box. "Heavens, Mom," she exclaimed, "Dad and I need our magic case!" Helen's mother and father looked at each other and smiled.

Be tolerant with one another and forgive one another whenever any of you has a complaint against someone else. You must forgive one another just as the Lord has forgiven you.

Colossians 3:13 TEV

Oh, Lord, forgive me for not forgiving others. Teach me to understand adults when they don't act like I want them to. Help me understand that things don't always go right for grown-up people either. Lord, be with us.

The Scholarship

"Margaret, throw your test paper in the waste-basket now!" Mr. Thompson, the history teacher, commanded. "I won't tolerate cheating in my class-room!"

Margaret's heart sank. It was true. She was cheating. She had copied two answers from Ora Lee, the girl who sat in front of her.

"You've disappointed me, Margaret!" Mr. Thompson went on to say. "To think that you, of all people, would cheat really disappoints me. You're the last person in this room I would have suspected!"

Mr. Thompson had good reason for saying that. Margaret was a Girl Scout, president of her class, and active in the young people's group at church. Everyone liked her. Her ambition was to be a nurse, and she was planning to take a class next summer to learn more about the nursing profession. Mr.

Thompson was even helping her apply for a scholarship.

Margaret had not wanted to cheat. But when everyone else did, the temptation was too great. Bill copied some answers from Jane who copied from Cheryl. On and on it went until everyone in class copied from one person and gave answers to another. But the rest of the class did not get caught—just Margaret.

Margaret's fingers trembled as she dropped her paper in the basket. *Why did I do it?* she wondered. She wanted to cry. If all her classmates had not been staring, she would have. But Margaret knew she had to look brave, even if she did not feel brave. Still, her chin quivered as she walked back to her desk and sat down.

"This means you'll get an F on your report card for the final six-weeks grade," Mr. Thompson continued, "and the scholarship is off."

The scholarship's off before it started! Margaret thought in dismay. She did not want her parents ever to find out about the F or the scholarship being called off, but the news scattered fast—so fast that by the time Margaret got home her mom already knew.

"How did you find out?" Margaret asked.

"Never mind how I found out, young lady," Mrs. Brawnson stormed. "When your father gets home, you're in trouble! I would never have thought you'd do such a thing!"

"But, Mom," Margaret began to protest, "everyone cheated."

"That's no excuse," Mrs. Brawnson stated.

When Margaret's father got home, he gave her

the worst punishment Margaret ever remembered getting. Mr. Brawnson said the only way to settle this would be for Margaret to visit Pastor Larry. "Anyone in junior high is too old to spank," Mr. Brawnson explained. "And you've got to have a punishment for the wrong you did."

Margaret wanted to disappear—forever. She did not want to be too old to spank, not now. *A spanking would be better than having to go see a minister*, Margaret thought. She wanted to die. *But if I die*, she thought, *I bet God wouldn't even let me go to heaven. Maybe I'd just go to that other place. My parents will never forgive me; neither will God.*

When report cards came, it was the final blow. Patsy, the class vice-president, raced to Margaret's locker. "Is it true what the other kids are saying?" Patsy asked. "Did you really get an F?"

Margaret slammed her locker door shut. "It's true," she confessed.

"Let me see," Patsy insisted, pulling the report card from Margaret's hand. "I can't believe Mr. Thompson would really give you an F. You always get A's."

Margaret pulled the report card back and put it inside a schoolbook. She slammed the book shut. "Let's talk about something else," she said.

"But what are you going to do?" Patsy asked.

"What can I do?" Margaret complained.

Patsy shrugged her shoulders. "I don't know," she said, "but there must be something."

"Ha!" Margaret laughed with sarcasm. "I suppose I could kill myself."

Margaret ran ahead of Patsy, down the hall, and

out the school door. The multicolored fall leaves of gold, red, and brown crushed beneath her feet.

Now that she was alone, Margaret pulled the report card from the book. How the F stuck out! It was more noticeable than the other grades. Margaret had never gotten an F until now. She wished she could erase it and put a B or C in its place. *I'd even settle for a D in this case*, Margaret thought. *Anything would be better than an F.*

Why did I cheat? Margaret kept wondering. She wished she could go back, start over. But it was too late.

In Pastor Larry's office, Margaret felt even worse. She hung her head and twisted her fingers together. She just wanted to get this consultation—or whatever you called it—over with.

"Your parents told me about your trouble at school," Pastor Larry began.

Margaret nodded her head.

"Want to tell me about it?" he asked.

Margaret took a deep breath. "Not really," she sighed.

Pastor Larry leaned back in his black office chair. "I think I understand," he said.

"You do?" Margaret asked, tears in her eyes.

"Yes, I think you feel as bad as I did when I cheated on an exam in geography class when I was in seventh grade."

Margaret jerked her head up, not knowing if she had heard right. *Pastor Larry? Cheat? In geography class?* She frowned.

"Oh, I know what you're thinking," Pastor Larry went on. "Christians aren't supposed to cheat. Especially pastors. Right?"

Margaret nodded her head. Pastor Larry leaned forward in his chair and pulled himself to the desk. "You see, Margaret," Pastor Larry began to explain, "I thought just copying a few answers wouldn't hurt that much. But naturally that was just as bad as if I'd copied every answer. What difference did it make? The point was I didn't take the test fairly. I got a better score than I should have."

"But I didn't get a better score. I got an—F," Margaret said, almost whispering.

"I'm sorry." Pastor Larry nodded.

"What did you get?" Margaret asked.

"An A. I didn't get caught."

"You were lucky," Margaret said.

"Was I really?" Pastor Larry asked. "I started feeling pretty guilty about that A. I felt like it didn't belong to me, which, of course, it didn't." Pastor Larry said even though he did not cheat again, he kept feeling guilty. "Years later, when I was in seminary, I got to feeling so bad about that A I wrote to my teacher and told her what I did."

"Then what did you get for your punishment?" Margaret asked.

Pastor Larry smiled. "That was the nicest part of all," he said. "I had no punishment."

"None?" Margaret asked.

"No, my teacher said she thought my conscience made me suffer enough. She forgave me," Pastor Larry said, smiling. "I was sort of like the prodigal son in the Bible. Remember, his father forgave him too, even though he had done wrong."

"But I'm no prodigal son. I've got a punishment," Margaret said softly. "I'm losing my chance to get a scholarship."

Pastor Larry nodded his head.

"The thing is, I wasn't the only one who cheated," Margaret said. "Everyone was copying answers."

"Umhummm," Pastor Larry leaned forward on his arms. "Your parents told me that too."

"What shall I do?" Margaret started sobbing. "I'm really not a bad kid. Am I?"

Pastor Larry smiled. "Of course you're not," he said. He told Margaret to bow her head; they would say a prayer. Pastor Larry prayed that Margaret be forgiven for cheating, that she was sorry and for the Lord to take care of everything so it would turn out all right.

Margaret could not believe everything would turn out all right. She could not forget the scholarship. She had wanted it so badly. Now it was gone, before she even had a chance to apply for it.

The next day, in history class, Patsy asked Mr. Thompson if the class could have a business meeting after school. Mr. Thompson was the class advisor. He checked his calendar and said that would be fine.

Margaret was puzzled. Since she was class president, she always knew when the class was having a business meeting. But no one told her about this. Why?

At the meeting, Patsy said they needed to talk about what happened the other day. The whole class, Patsy informed Mr. Thompson, had cheated. Mr. Thompson raised his eyebrows.

"I didn't know that," he said.

"We know you didn't, and we're all sorry," Patsy said. "We feel bad about Margaret's scholarship.

Margaret's the only one that got punished because she's the only one that got caught."

Mr. Thompson studied the class. He asked everyone that cheated to raise his or her hand. Slowly, one by one, all hands rose.

"Yes, I see what you mean," Mr. Thompson said, peering over his gold-framed glasses. He gave the class a lecture on cheating, explaining why it was wrong. "It's a crutch," Mr. Thompson warned. "Don't start using it, or you'll find you can't get along without cheating on a few questions every time you take a test. It's habit-forming, like taking drugs. Remember, the only person you really cheat is yourself."

Mr. Thompson paced the floor, his hands behind his back. "Tell you what I'm going to do," he finally said. "I'm going to give you another test today. The other one won't count. This test will be on the same subject but different questions. And this test *will* count. No cheating! Understood?"

The students nodded their heads. Later, when Margaret turned in her test paper, Mr. Thompson picked it up and studied it for a moment.

"Looks like you did a great job on this without cheating," he said. Mr. Thompson put his hand on Margaret's shoulder. "By the way, how would you like to fill out the application papers for that scholarship now?"

Margaret smiled and gasped at the same time. "You mean—you mean, I can—you've forgiven me?" she asked.

Mr. Thompson smiled. "I've forgiven you," he said. "But let this be your lesson. Promise not to cheat again, and I'll help you apply for the scholarship."

Margaret nodded, smiling through her tears. She knew now why Pastor Larry liked the story of the prodigal son.

> No more lying, then! Everyone must tell the truth to his fellow believers, because we are all members together in the body of Christ.
>
> Ephesians 4:25 TEV

Teach me to always tell the truth, Lord. Help me not to cheat. When I am tempted to cheat, come to me and give me strength.

The Swimming Race

Betty felt like her parents did not notice her. When her older sister, Louise, sang in the church choir, her parents said, "My, Louise, you have a lovely voice." Of course, Betty never sang in the choir. She was not old enough, and besides, her voice cracked.

Thomas, Betty's younger brother, was a genius. He always got A's in school. When he brought his report card home, Betty's parents said, "My, Tom, your grades are great." Of course, Betty never got all A's. In fact, she seldom got an A. Even the couple of B's she got once in awhile got lost in the crowd of C's on her report card.

The situation became worse as Louise got popular with boys. When a date called for Louise, Betty's parents later said to each other, "My, did you notice how nice and short his hair was?" And Thomas gained more recognition every day after he made the football team. Betty's parents were always asking Thomas when the next game was. "We sure don't want to miss it," they would say.

"I'm not good at anything," Betty confided to Flora, her best friend, one day.

"Everyone's good at something," Flora began to argue.

"Not me," Betty said. "There's nothing I can do better than anyone else."

Both girls sat on the front porch of Betty's home. Betty cupped her chin in the palms of her hands. "If my parents aren't talking about how well Louise sings, they're talking about what a great football player Tom is," Betty said. "Sometimes I can hardly stand to listen. Sometimes I've even wondered if I'm adopted."

"*Adopted?*" Flora screeched. "Why, Betty Ferguson, where'd you ever get a silly notion like that? How could you be adopted? You've got your mother's dark hair, blue eyes, and small nose and mouth. You can't be adopted if you look like your mother in all those ways."

Betty thought a minute. Flora had a good point. People were always telling Betty she looked like her mother. "Why, your voices even sound the same over the telephone," they would say. Except, of course, Mrs. Ferguson's voice did not crack. In reality, Betty knew Flora was right. She was not adopted.

"I guess what I mean to say is I *feel* adopted," Betty said. Flora cupped her chin in the palms of her hands like Betty.

"Well," Flora sighed, "I guess I see where that would be a problem. I mean, it's fine to be adopted.

But it's bad news if you feel adopted when you're not adopted."

Betty got up from the porch and walked to the hammock a few feet away. She sat on the edge, swinging back and forth. "Yeah, I have to get good at something quick," she said. "I want my parents to notice me."

Flora stretched her arms around her legs. "Don't forget, you play the piano," she said.

Betty stopped swinging in the hammock and flipped her hands over her eyes. "Don't remind me," Betty groaned.

"Why not?" Flora asked.

"Because Louise plays better than I do," she groaned again.

"Are you sure?" Flora asked. "Aren't you just imagining the worst?"

Betty got up from the hammock. She put her hands on her chest, spreading her fingers apart. "Me?" she exclaimed. "Imagining the worst? OK, you tell me why it is when Louise plays the piano, my parents request songs, and when I play, they ask if I have any homework."

"But I like the way you play the piano," Flora insisted.

Betty grinned. That was one thing she loved about Flora. Flora always tried to cheer her up—even when things looked as grim as they did now.

"You're a good friend," Betty said, "but be honest. If you were judge at a piano recital, and Louise played *Waltz of the Flowers* and then I played *Waltz of the Flowers*, who would you pick to win?"

Flora giggled. "That's a silly question. You don't

even know *Waltz of the Flowers,* and Louise plays that song extra well."

Betty sighed. "Flora, remember when you were over at my house yesterday and you sat beside me for 30 minutes until I finished practicing the piano?"

"Uh-huh, so?"

"So, what do you think I was struggling through?" Betty asked, shouting.

Flora squirmed on the porch, hung her chin, and whispered, *"Waltz of the Flowers?"*

"You got it!" Betty said. "Now, tell me I don't have a problem!"

Flora frowned for a minute. "But Louise is three years older," she finally said. "Don't you suppose her fingers are a lot stronger than yours?"

Betty studied her hands and shook her head. "I doubt it," Betty answered, "but I will admit one thing, Flora—you consider every angle. Have you ever thought about law school?"

Flora snapped her fingers. "That gives me an idea! Why not become the first woman president?" she asked.

Betty said that was an excellent suggestion, but it was too long to wait. "By that time, I'm not sure my parents will still be alive," Betty explained. "Besides, I want them to notice me now, like they notice Tom and Louise. I want action now."

Flora snapped her fingers again, and she jumped from the porch. "That's it!" she exclaimed. "That's it!"

"What's it?" Betty asked, puzzled.

"Action!" Flora shouted. "That's exactly what you can give your parents!"

"But how?" Betty asked. "Break a leg? Or an arm maybe?"

Flora giggled. "No, silly. What I mean is, the Girl's Club is having a swimming meet. There are going to be swimming races for girls of all ages, and the first place winner in every category gets a trophy. Even if you don't win first prize, everyone gets a ribbon just for participating."

Betty cupped her chin in her hands again and thought. "Swimming, huh?" she muttered. The more she thought about it, the more it seemed like a good idea. Tom was a boy, so naturally he could not enter, and Louise wouldn't want to—Louise was afraid of the water. And a ribbon! Betty knew just where she could hang it, right on the mantel above the fireplace, in the den, for everyone to see. The next thing Betty knew she was asking Flora if she would like to go swimming that afternoon.

During the next few days, Betty swam, swam, swam. She practiced different dives and swimming strokes. Then the big day came. Betty's parents went with her to the swimming meet. So did Louise and Thomas.

"I'll get a ribbon today just for being in the race," Betty said, smiling. "Can I hang it on the mantel when we get home?"

"We'll see," her father answered.

But Betty did not get a ribbon. Instead, when Betty and her family went home, the shiny, gold, first-place trophy was set on the mantel. Everyone stepped back to look at it.

"I think that's the perfect spot for it," Betty's mother said.

"So do I," her father added, grinning. "That way everyone can see it."

"You must feel good," Louise said.

Thomas slapped Betty on the back. "Yeah, not bad," he commented.

Betty smiled. Everyone was noticing her, and it felt good.

> Do not neglect the spiritual gift that is in you. . . . Practice these things and devote yourself to them, in order that your progress may be seen by all.
>
> 1 Timothy 4:14-15 TEV

Oh, Lord, teach me I am not forgotten when I think I'm not talented. Help me to use the special talents you gave me.

The Horrible Speech

Laura Hesper did not want to go to school. Generally she was excited about Thursdays because of English, her favorite class. But this Thursday was different. She had to give a speech.

How Laura dreaded it! It was not because she was unprepared for the speech. As a matter of fact, she had spent all week organizing, writing, and rewriting the speech. She recited it hundreds of times to her stuffed animals on her bed. Of course, Laura did not mind presenting the speech to a stuffed animal audience. But she did mind giving a speech in front of her classmates. She was scared.

Maybe, Laura thought, *I could stay home and pretend I'm sick.* But the more Laura thought about the idea, the more she did not like it. If she stayed home, Laura realized, her English instructor would make her give the speech when she came back to school. *I might as well get it over with,* Laura thought. *Besides, I'm not really sick.*

As Laura walked to school, her short, brown curls tossed in the wind. She tried not to think about the speech, but it kept popping into her mind. Ever since Mrs. Bolt assigned the speech, Laura had thought about it. *What if I get so scared I lose my voice?* Laura kept wondering. *Worse yet, what if I faint?*

By 9:00, the time for her English class, Laura was a nervous wreck. She twisted her hands and fumbled through her notes. Her heart beat heavy strokes. Her legs felt limp and she was short of breath.

Marilyn was the first classmate to give a speech. She was a good friend. Laura waited for Marilyn to make some mistake or fumble over some words. Laura thought if Marilyn goofed a little, then she would not be so frightened. But Marilyn did all the right things. Her voice was calm, her hands did not shake, and she smiled.

Doesn't anyone else feel the same way I do? Laura wondered. *Isn't anyone else scared to give a speech?*

When Marilyn finished her speech, the class applauded. "That was very good," Mrs. Bolt said. "Let's see. Who's next? How about a volunteer?" There was silence. Mrs. Bolt's eyes rolled over her grade book. "Let's just go down my list then," Mrs. Bolt said. "Al, will you please be next?"

Laura's heart beat faster and her mouth was dry. She knew she was next in line after Al Gripps. Like Marilyn, Al's voice was calm and he appeared not to be scared. When Al concluded his speech, Laura was dizzy. "Very good, Al," Mrs. Bolt remarked, "you

just may be a good student to try out for the debate team."

Mrs. Bolt returned to her grade book. She looked at Laura and smiled. "You're next," she said, nodding to Laura.

Laura got her notes and went to the front of the room. Her heart was beating so hard now that she had a headache. When she looked at her notes, the words moved to and fro. As she spoke, her voice shook and her entire body trembled.

After Laura finished the horrible speech, Mrs. Bolt did it again. She assigned more speeches! These speeches, Mrs. Bolt explained, were to be panel discussions. "That means I want three or four of you to be on a panel together and present a discussion," Mrs. Bolt said. "So start thinking about who you'd like to work with. I'll let you pick your own partners."

After class Laura started walking towards Marilyn. Marilyn was huddled in a corner with Maureen and Claire. With her hands on her cheeks, Marilyn exclaimed, "Wasn't that just the most horrible speech you ever heard!" The words stabbed Laura. She turned around and rushed down the hall. Marilyn called to her, but she went on. She felt embarrassed and ashamed now of her horrible speech. She did not want to talk to anyone now—especially Marilyn! Marilyn gave such a good speech. Even if they were good friends, Marilyn would never want Laura on her panel discussion. Laura knew that now.

Laura rushed to her next class. She was safe from Marilyn until lunch hour. Surely she could think of some way to escape from Marilyn by then. There was no way Laura was going to sit through lunch with Marilyn and hear about the good speech Marilyn gave and the horrible one she gave.

When lunch hour came, Laura had a plan. She could go down the west stairway, through the social studies room, and out the gym door. That way she would probably be last in the cafeteria line and Marilyn would not find her.

The lunch bell rang. Laura was the first one out the hallway. She raced down the stairway.

"Hold it, young lady!" Mr. Johnson, the social studies teacher, said. "Just where are you going? To a fire? You'd better slow down. You know you're not supposed to run in the school building!"

Laura hung her head. "Yes, sir," she muttered. *Rats!* she thought. *Why did he have to be standing there today?* She continued on her way, but when she got to the gym door, she could not open it. It was stuck. She pushed hard against the door with her shoulders. When it opened, Marilyn, Claire, and Maureen were facing her!

"Are you detectives or something?" Laura snapped.

"Why are you running away from us?" Marilyn asked. "We've been trying to track you down all morning. Don't you want to talk to us? Don't you like us anymore?"

"I've been busy," Laura said, ignoring the questions.

"We want you on our panel," Maureen said.

"Panel?" Laura asked, pretending she did not know what panel Maureen meant.

"You know," Claire said, "for the panel discussion for English class. We were all talking this morning and thought it'd be fun for all of us to give a discussion on sewing."

"Yeah," Marilyn added, "and since you've made some of your clothes you sure could help us a lot. I do hope you're not planning to be with someone else. Can you come over to my house tonight? We're all getting together to practice."

"But—but—I heard what you said, Marilyn!" Laura finally stammered.

"What did I say?" Marilyn asked, frowning.

"How—well, what a horrible speech I gave," Laura answered.

"She wasn't talking about you, silly," Claire giggled.

"She wasn't?" Laura asked.

"No," Maureen giggled too.

Marilyn curled herself in a knot and laughed. "I meant *my* speech!" she exclaimed.

Laura stared at Marilyn. "But you gave such a good speech," she said.

Marilyn smiled. "Thanks, Laura, you're such a good friend. But let me tell you, I was scared!"

"You scared?" Laura asked, shaking her head. "I can't believe it."

"Didn't you hear my knees shake? They knocked against each other so hard I thought I'd end up with bruises. Look! Here's how they went." Marilyn bounced her knees together in jerky movements.

The girls giggled. "Believe me, I'm scared to give my speech tomorrow," Claire said.

"You want to know how scared I am to give my speech?" Maureen asked.

Laura nodded.

"I'm so scared maybe you all better arrange to have an ambulance on hand—just in case," Maureen said, chuckling.

Laura smiled. "Sure, I'll come over to your house tonight, Marilyn," she said.

> To have faith is to be sure of the things we hope for, to be certain of the things we cannot see.
>
> Hebrews 11:1 TEV

Oh, Lord, help me when I get scared. Give me courage to do my best, and, if I do goof up, help me try better next time.

The Prettiest Dress

Malinda wanted a new dress for Easter. She even knew which dress she wanted. Every day, on her way home from school, Malinda walked an extra three blocks just to see the dress. It was on display in the window of Becker's Department Store. It was a blue paisley in a soft, woven fabric. Malinda knew the dress would look good on her. It had a high collar, short sleeves, an empire waist, and a slightly gathered skirt—very stylish, very chic, Malinda thought.

"Mom, let's go shopping," Malinda said one day after she came bouncing in from school.

"Not today," Mrs. Gibson replied.

"Aw, Mom, come on," Malinda said, "why not?"

"Because we're having company for dinner," Mrs. Gibson answered.

"Do they have kids?" Malinda wanted to know.

Mrs. Gibson smiled, saying she was sorry but no they did not have any children. Malinda threw her school books on the kitchen table. It was going to be one of those boring evenings, she thought. All grown-up company.

"But I want you to see the dress I want for Easter," Malinda went on.

Mrs. Gibson stopped frosting the chocolate layer cake for a moment and looked at Malinda. "Dress?" she asked. "What dress?"

Malinda explained she wanted the dress on display in Becker's Department Store. "You'll like it. It's washable," she said.

"How do you know that?" Mrs. Gibson asked.

"I looked at the price tag one day on the way home from school. I walk by there every day just to see it, Mom. It's got to be the prettiest dress in the whole world."

Mrs. Gibson started frosting the cake again. "You say that about every dress you like," she said.

Malinda sighed and said this dress was different, this dress really was the prettiest dress in the whole world. She bent over the table and scooped some frosting from the bowl with her finger. Mrs. Gibson handed Malinda a spoon. "Here," she said, "use this to lick the frosting." Malinda took the spoon and began scooping the frosting from the bowl. Chocolate was her favorite.

"Now, about the dress," Malinda's mother said, wiping her hands on a paper towel. "I'm afraid you can't have one for Easter this year."

"What?" Malinda shouted, dropping the spoon from her mouth. "But I get a new dress every year for Easter."

Mrs. Gibson smiled. "I know, and you also get new shoes and a nice, new purse too."

"So why can't I get a new dress?" Malinda asked, her blue eyes widening.

Mrs. Gibson sat beside Malinda. "Honey, sometimes parents just can't give their children everything they'd like to, and I'm afraid this is one of those times," she said.

Malinda could not understand. All she was asking for was a new dress. It was not like she wanted a stereo or a 10-speed bike. "Heavens, Mom," she said, "I'd wear it a lot. You won't have to see me in my blue jeans all the time if I can have it. Please, Mom. Just come and see it. I know you'll love it."

"But it's not a question of whether I'll like it or not," Mrs. Gibson said.

Malinda still did not understand. Usually that was the big problem when she and her mother went shopping—to find something they both liked. What Mrs. Gibson thought looked nice on Malinda, Malinda usually could not stand. But this dress, Malinda just knew, her Mom would like too. So why couldn't she have it? She wanted to know.

Mrs. Gibson sighed and poured herself a cup of tea. "Well, you've heard about inflation. Everything's so high-priced these days," she began.

"But this dress is cheap," Malinda interrupted.

"How do you know that?" Mrs. Gibson asked.

"I saw the price tag. It's on a special sale, only 20 dollars," Malinda answered.

Mrs. Gibson raised her eyebrows. "*Only* 20 dollars?" she asked, shaking her head. "To think when I was your age—what a dress cost then—"

"I know, I know," Malinda said. She didn't want to

hear another one of those kids-sure-don't-know-how-lucky-they-are-these-days lectures. "You're always saying I wear jeans too much. I should think you'd be glad to buy it," Malinda went on.

"All I'm trying to tell you is this year you can't have a new dress for Easter," Mrs. Gibson said. "Remember, you just got new shoes and a new purse. That's plenty."

Plenty? Malinda could not believe what she was hearing. Every girl in church would have a new dress for Easter. What was her mom thinking? *Doesn't she realize how important the blue paisley dress is to me?* Malinda wondered.

"But, Mom, I don't have a thing to wear for Easter Sunday," Malinda kept complaining.

Mrs. Gibson sighed again and got up to start dinner. "You have a closet full of pretty dresses, and yet you say you don't have a thing to wear," she said.

Pretty dresses? Malinda thought. *How old-fashioned can Mom get?* They were old dresses. No one wore an old dress to church on Easter Sunday. The more Malinda thought about it, the more she decided she had to have the blue paisley dress. But when she asked her father about it, it was the same story. "We just can't afford it now," he said.

The closer it got to Easter, the more Malinda dreamed about the dress. She even showed it to her mom one day when they happened to be walking by the store. But her mother would not let Malinda go in to try on the dress even then.

"Why not?" Malinda asked.

"There's just no point in it if I know we can't buy it anyway," her mother said. "Besides, I have a surprise for you."

A surprise? Malinda thought, *I bet Mom's planning to buy the dress and surprise me!*

Every day Malinda kept walking the three extra blocks on the way home from school to see the dress. Then on Friday, Good Friday in fact, it happened. The dress was not in the window! Malinda ran all the way home. She just knew her mom had bought the dress for her.

"Can I see my surprise now?" Malinda asked when she got home.

"Why, yes," Mrs. Gibson said, smiling, "as a matter of fact, you can. I just finished it."

Mrs. Gibson took Malinda into her sewing room and showed her the surprise. Malinda's heart fell. The surprise was the dress she had worn last year for Easter. Mrs. Gibson had sewed extra wide white lace around the waistline and sleeves.

Doesn't Mom realize lace is ancient history? Malinda wondered. Tears stung her eyes, but she dared not cry.

"Well, how do you like it?" Mrs. Gibson asked.

A lump stuck in Malinda's throat. "Fine," she muttered.

Malinda wished she would get sick Easter Sunday. That way no one would know she did not get a new dress for Easter. That way no one would see her wear her old pink dress. . . .

On Easter Sunday Malinda took a deep breath and pulled at the pink dress before going into her Sunday school room. Even if the lace was ancient history, Malinda tried to count her blessings. *Maybe this way no one will notice it's the same old thing I wore last year*, she thought.

When she walked into the room, Malinda had another surprise. There sat her friend Vicki in the blue paisley dress! When Malinda thought about it for a moment, she realized she should have figured it out for herself. Naturally Vicki would get the dress. Vicki always wore the prettiest, most stylish clothes.

Vicki ran to Malinda. "Wow!" Vicki exclaimed, "aren't you the lucky one!"

Malinda frowned. "What?" she asked.

"Your dress," Vicki said, "where did you ever find such a pretty dress? All my mother and I could find was this blue paisley. I hate blue paisley!"

For a moment Malinda thought she must not be wearing the pink dress. She glanced down, just to make sure. "But I wore this last year," she confessed.

Vicki studied the dress. "Yes, maybe you did. But I don't remember it that well. Besides, isn't there something different about it?"

Malinda shrugged her shoulders. "My mom sewed the lace on," she said.

Vicki shook her head. "That's it! I sure do like it. Lace is in now, you know."

Malinda did not know, but she said nothing. She looked at her pink dress again. Now that she thought about it, the lace did give it a stylish look.

> . . . I tell you not to worry about the food you need to stay alive or about the clothes you need for your body. Life is much more important than food, and the body much more important than clothes.
>
> Luke 12:22-23 TEV

78

Oh, Lord, teach me not to want the things I cannot have. Let me be happy in knowing I have you. That is all I need.

Winning Entry of the Science Fair

"You'll never win the Science Fair with that solar system," Jennifer told her sister Reita.

"Of course I will!" Reita exclaimed. "This is bound to win."

"Ha! Who are you kidding?" Jennifer asked, peering into the clear plastic case. "Your planets aren't hanging right."

Reita stepped back to study her planets. "Just what exactly is wrong with the way my planets are hanging?" Reita asked.

"Pluto is too close to Uranus, there's too much space between Mercury and the sun, and Venus is up too high," Jennifer answered.

"Just when did you become an expert on planets?" Reita asked. Reita swirled her tongue around her lips as she started gluing Saturn to a string in the case.

"I wouldn't put Saturn that near the edge of your

case, either, if I were you," Jennifer advised. "Move it over a couple of inches. Say, you know what you need is a scale. I'll let you use my calculator to figure it, if you like."

Reita's fingers slipped from the Styrofoam ball which was her Saturn. It landed on the floor, hitting the blue shag carpet with the glued side down. "Well, you're not me!" Reita shouted. "And can't you see I'm busy?"

"Sorry, I was only trying to help."

"I don't need your help!" Reita shouted again.

"OK. But I still say if you'd put your solar system on a scale, you'd have a better chance of winning something," Jennifer added, walking out of the room.

Ha! Reita thought to herself. *Just wait. I'll show that big smarty. Wait until I bring my winning trophy home. Then she'll see I know what I'm doing.*

More than anything, Reita wanted her entry to win. She loved to win. Reita was always entering a contest or race. She had won piano contests, spelling bees, swimming races, and essay-writing contests. Her room was filled with ribbons, trophies, and certificates.

But Reita had no science awards in her collection of honors. That was because she hadn't known about the Science Fair until this year. She was glad one of her classmates, Pam, had given her the contest rule sheets.

Reita had worked for three weeks on her entry, the solar system. She had bought Styrofoam balls in different sizes to make the different planets, and she had colored them with bright colors. Today she was working extra hard, putting the final touches on the planets. She attached them to her display cabinet by hanging each planet from a length of fine thread.

When Reita finished gluing Saturn in place, she put on her pajamas, hopped in bed, and said a prayer. *Please, Lord,* she prayed, *help me win first place or second or third. Just help me win.* She prayed that same prayer for all the contests she entered. Reita was excited. Even second and third place winners in the Science Fair got money and a nice ribbon. She looked around the room to see where she could hang the ribbon.

I know, Reita thought, *I'll hang my ribbon over Jennifer's picture of her boyfriend. That way she's sure to see it. Or, if I get first place, I'll just set my trophy in the hall for Jennifer to trip over.*

The next morning Reita jumped out of bed. She hurried through breakfast. It was the day of the Science Fair at last.

When Reita got to school with her solar system, Pam met her at the door. "Hi," Pam said, holding a large scroll of newsprint. "Need some help?"

"Yeah," Reita answered, "where do I put my masterpiece?"

Pam led Reita to the table where the solar systems were displayed.

"Boy, that looks neat," Pam said as she studied Reita's entry. The scroll, Pam explained to Reita, was her entry. Pam taped it to the wall. On the plain newsprint paper, Pam had colored the solar system with crayons. Reita was surprised when she saw it; she thought it was nothing special.

There were 50 entries in all. There were more solar system displays besides Reita's and Pam's entries.

There were also entries on volcanoes, telescope making, and rock and bug collections.

The three judges walked into the room. They were introduced by the president of the PTA. One judge was a medical technologist, one taught science in the high school, and one studied the stars with a telescope for a hobby.

The three judges walked about the room, surveying each entry. They asked questions of the students who had entered their projects.

Reita's stomach curled in knots when the judges approached the solar system table. They started studying the solar system entries, one by one. One judge nodded his head when he got to Reita's entry. "Nice," he commented. Another judge smiled. The third judge asked Reita how far Jupiter was from the sun. Reita's face reddened. She confessed she did not know.

"Can anyone at this table tell me?" she asked.

For a moment the room was silent. Then Pam pointed to her chart. "I can tell you with my chart," Pam said. "I made a scale."

The judge walked to Pam's chart and nodded.

"Let's see," Pam began, pointing to the chart. "Here it is. Jupiter is 778,300,000 kilometers from the sun. And look, the day is only about 9 hours and 55 minutes long on Jupiter. And, besides that, Jupiter's the largest planet in our solar system."

The judge turned and motioned for the other judges to join her. All three judges assembled around Pam's chart. They asked Pam questions about the scale she used for her solar system.

"You must have read a lot of books for this project," one judge said.

Pam folded her arms, closed her eyes for a couple of seconds, and sighed, "Let's see. I read *Planets in Outer Space, The Solar System, Is There Plant Life on Mars?, Why Does Saturn Have Rings?*, and another book called *Planets, Stars, and Moons*."

Reita's eyes widened. She was impressed. No wonder Pam knew so much about the solar system.

The judges took a break to eat donuts and drink coffee. Then they sat down at the judges' table and started scoring the final points for each entry on their score sheets.

Reita went over to Pam. "You sure do know a lot about the solar system," Reita said.

Pam shrugged her shoulders. "Aw, it's easy if you read some books and make a scale."

Reita nodded her head and sighed. "My big sister warned me," Reita said. "She told me to make a scale, but I wouldn't listen."

Pam smiled. "It's not always easy to listen to big sisters," she said. "I've got one too."

Reita smiled back. Pam sure was nice.

Mrs. Lender, the PTA president, stood up and tapped a spoon on a glass. "May I have your attention, please?" she said. "The judges are ready to announce the winners."

The third place winner was a boy who entered a clay model of a volcano. Second place went to a girl who loved bugs. She had a wide collection, ranging from a small beetle to a large dragonfly.

"Now I know this is the moment you're all waiting for," the judge said, smiling, "but before I announce our first place winner, I'd like to say all the entries were good this year, even better than last year. So, let's give everyone who entered something here today a hand."

After the loud applause had died down, the judge cleared his throat. "Now the first place winner is from our solar system table," he began.

Pam and Reita looked at each other and smiled. "Suppose it's one of us?" Pam asked.

"I don't know," Reita answered, taking a deep breath. "But this is more exciting than watching the Academy Awards on television!"

"The first place winner is—Pam Kitson!"

Pam and Reita threw their arms around each other. "Looks like yours was the best," Reita said, smiling.

"Thanks," Pam said. "Want to come over to my house for pizza? We'll celebrate together."

"Sure," Reita said. She felt like celebrating. Even if she didn't win the prize, she had made a good friend.

> Surely you know that many run-
> ners take part in a race, but only
> one of them wins the prize.
>
> 1 Corinthians 9:24 TEV

When I enter a contest, Lord, help me realize only one person can win first prize. When I don't win, help me to be a good sport. Even if my chances of winning are slim, help me do my best anyway.

Karen's Diets

"Listen, Georgia, why doesn't anyone like me?" Karen asked.

Georgia played with a strand of her hair and leaned against the wall. "Well, I'm not sure," she sighed, "but Bobby says it's because you're so fat."

So that's it, Karen thought. *That's why when everyone goes for pizza after school, no one asks me to come along. Or when my class plays kick ball at recess, I'm always left behind, puffing at the other end of the field.*

"You mean, that's why when the other girls get together for a slumber party, I'm never invited?" Karen asked.

Georgia shrugged her shoulders. "Could be," she said.

Karen knew she weighed too much. She weighed 90 pounds. Dr. Smithson said Karen should weigh about 70 pounds. Still, Karen did not like it when Georgia said that. And just who did Bobby think he was anyway?

Karen was so upset when she got home from school, she did not eat her usual snack—a bowl of potato chips, some cheese slices, a candy bar, and a Coke. Instead, Karen sneaked in the cookie jar and ate eight chocolate chip cookies. Karen always ate a lot when she was upset. Of course, she ate a lot when she was not upset too. That was the problem. Karen ate too much every day.

After Karen ate the cookies, she decided to go on a diet. That evening, at the dinner table, Karen made the announcement.

"I've decided to go on a diet," Karen said, sitting straight in her chair.

"Again?" Karen's brother, Scott, asked.

"This time I mean business!" Karen exclaimed.

"Yeah, just like last time," Scott said, grinning. "Remember? You gained six pounds!"

There were times Karen wanted to hit Scott right in the middle of his face. If her parents had not been at the dinner table, she would have. Instead, she continued to eat quietly. But she did not eat much for supper since she was dieting—and especially since Scott was watching with his beady blue eyes.

After Karen helped with the dishes, she got hungry. She looked at the cookie jar. *Just one more cookie won't hurt*, Karen thought. When no one was looking, she reached into the jar, grabbed a cookie, and ate it before anyone saw her. But before she went to bed, she was hungry again.

"Have a glass of skim milk or fruit juice," her mother suggested.

That sounded good to Karen. She had both.

The next day at school, in the cafeteria, Karen decided to ask for a special tray. Special trays were given to kids who needed special diets. Karen got in the lunch line behind Gary. He always got a special tray because he was diabetic.

Karen was all ready to ask for a special tray, but then she noticed Gary's tray. It did not have a piece of chocolate cake on it like the regular trays. And, instead of grilled cheese sandwiches, Gary's tray had tuna fish salad. Karen hated tuna fish. But how she loved chocolate cake and grilled cheese sandwiches.

"What can I get for you today?" one of the cooks asked Karen.

"Um, just my usual lunch tray," Karen said.

The cook handed Karen a tray with chocolate cake and cheese sandwiches. *Just having a regular tray this once won't hurt,* Karen tried to convince herself. *Besides, I won't eat much for supper.*

That evening Mrs. Jones was happy when Karen said she did not want dessert. "I'm pleased you're sticking to your diet this time," Karen's mother said, smiling.

Actually Karen did not mind turning down dessert. It was raisin and rice pudding. If there was one thing Karen did not like, it was raisin and rice pudding.

At school the next day, Karen asked for a special tray. She asked for another the next day. But on Friday, when there was cherry cobbler for dessert, Karen asked for a regular tray. *How can I miss cherry cobbler,* Karen wondered, *when it's my favorite? Besides, just having a regular tray twice a week won't hurt.*

Saturday morning Karen jumped out of bed. She

could hardly wait to weigh herself. She had dieted for nearly a whole week now. She wondered how many pounds she had lost. But when she stepped on the scale, she groaned.

"What is it?" Mrs. Jones asked.

"I've gained two pounds this week!" Karen exclaimed, "and I'm on a diet!"

Mrs. Jones put her arm around Karen. "That reminds me," she said, raising her eyebrows, "who got into the cookie jar?"

Karen hung her head, her face reddening. "But, Mom, I didn't think one cookie just once in a while would hurt. Do you suppose that's why I gained two pounds?"

Mrs. Jones nodded her head.

Karen did not know what to do. She stared at herself in the mirror. She did not like the way she looked. She was mad. She wished she had not eaten the cookies and the chocolate cake and the grilled cheese sandwiches and all the other high-calorie foods.

At Sunday school the next day, Karen felt even worse when she saw her teacher, Mrs. Jameson. Mrs. Jameson, who had the slimmest waist, was carrying a donut and a glass of juice.

"I don't think it's fair the way some people are thin and others aren't," Karen blurted to Mrs. Jameson.

"I beg your pardon?" Mrs. Jameson asked. She smiled and sat beside Karen.

"It's not fair the way I can't eat," Karen said.

"But who says you can't eat?" Mrs. Jameson said. "Everyone needs nourishment."

Karen flipped her hands in the air and sighed. "When I eat I gain weight like an elephant," Karen complained. "I just look at fudge candy and gain

92

weight. I just look at chocolate cake and gain weight. I just look at pumpkin pie and gain weight."

"No one gains weight from *looking* at food," Mrs. Jameson said. "People gain weight only when they eat it."

Karen sighed again. "All I know is I was on a diet this week and I gained two pounds!"

Mrs. Jameson picked up the Bible that was on the table. "Tell me, Karen, have you ever tried God's diet?" she asked.

"If it's the one where you eat tuna fish and grapefruit, forget it," Karen said. "I don't like that diet."

Mrs. Jameson chuckled and said that was not the diet she meant. Then she opened the Bible and showed Karen different scripture verses that showed God wants people to eat a variety of nutritious foods. Karen frowned.

"Karen, do you know what I do on other days than Sunday?" Mrs. Jameson asked. Karen shook her head. Mrs. Jameson explained she was a dietitian.

"But you don't need to go on a diet," Karen said. "You're thin already."

"Thank you, Karen, but being a dietitian means I plan diet menus for people. I work in a hospital. If you want me to, I could plan a diet for you so you could lose weight."

"If it's the bread diet, forget it," Karen said. "I gained three pounds on that in a week."

"No, it's not the bread diet," Mrs. Jameson said, smiling. "This diet would have lots of different and good foods that God likes you to eat. Do you want to try it?"

Karen thought. She wondered how it would feel to wear a dress with a waistband, or a skirt and sweater.

She wore sloppy, loose clothes with elastic waistbands that expanded when she gained weight. After Karen thought about her clothes, she agreed to try God's diet.

Mrs. Jameson said she would talk to Karen's parents and the school cooks.

"Now remember, when I give the school cooks your menu, it means you'll have to take a special tray every day," Mrs. Jameson stated.

Karen groaned.

"But also remember," Mrs. Jameson went on, "I'll say a prayer for you every day. You can lose weight with God's help."

A few days later, Mrs. Jameson came to Karen's house. She showed Karen and Mrs. Jones the diet. When Karen looked at the menu sheet, she knew something must be wrong. She thought the diet sounded good!

"Look!" Karen exclaimed, "it's even got mashed potatoes. I love mashed potatoes!"

Mrs. Jameson raised her finger. "But what do you eat on your mashed potatoes, Karen?" she asked.

Karen shrugged her shoulders. "Just butter and gravy," Karen said.

"Now take another look at your menu," Mrs. Jameson said. "I made a special note you're not to have anything on the potatoes."

"How about sour cream and bacon bits?" Karen asked.

"Nothing," Mrs. Jameson said, shaking her head.

"I knew there was a catch," Karen said.

Mrs. Jameson and Mrs. Jones both told Karen she could do it.

"I'll pray for you too, honey," Mrs. Jones said. "And I'll stop buying potato chips and making cookies."

"But, Mom," Karen protested, "I don't want you to do that."

Mrs. Jameson patted Karen's back. "Listen, Karen, if you want to lose weight, you must forget about cookies and other high-calorie foods that don't have many vitamins. Just develop self-control. Whenever you want a cookie, try eating a stick of celery or a carrot or an apple."

The first diet day, Karen dreamed of banana splits, pecan pie, and chocolate cake. The second day, she thought of cookies, potato chips, and Cokes. But by the third day, Karen was so hungry the celery and carrot sticks started tasting good.

At the end of the week, Karen jumped on the scale. "Mom, come here quick! I've lost two pounds!" Karen shouted. "Come here quick and see me before I gain it back."

"That's great," Mrs. Jones said, hugging Karen. "That's a beginning. I've even lost a couple pounds myself since I quit baking cookies."

After three more weeks, Karen lost another six pounds. Another three weeks passed. Karen lost eight more pounds. Dr. Smithson was pleased. So was Mrs. Jameson. So was Mrs. Jones. So was Karen!

"Hey, what diet are you on this time, kid?" Karen's brother asked one night at the dinner table. "It's working!"

Karen was so happy. Because she lost so much weight, her mother bought her two new pair of slacks —with real waistbands, not elastic. One pair was pink and the other pair was purple, Karen's favorite colors.

Dr. Smithson and Mrs. Jameson said Karen only

had four more pounds to lose. Then one day at school, Georgia and Lynn, another classmate, met Karen in the hall.

"Hey, did you see your name on the list?" Georgia asked Karen.

"What list?" Karen asked.

"The list for the spring dress style show," Lynn explained. "The home economics teacher picked you to be one of the models."

"Me?" Karen exclaimed. "You're kidding!" A wide smile spread across her face.

"No," Georgia answered. "Lynn and I are going to be models too. Isn't it great?"

"Can everyone come to my house after school?" Lynn asked. "We could start practicing how to walk like real models do."

"Sure, I'll come," Karen said. She decided then God's diet was the best diet of all.

> Don't you know that your body is the temple of the Holy Spirit, who lives in you and who was given to you by God? You do not belong to yourselves, but to God.
> 1 Corinthians 6:19 TEV

Oh, Lord, junk food surrounds me wherever I go. Department stores are filled with candy, bubble gum, and soda pop. Help me to eat only the foods my body needs.

Rules, Rules, and More Rules

Cindy was fed up with rules. Every time she turned around, she heard a rule. "Cindy, you didn't make your bed," her father would say. "You're to make your bed every morning. That's a rule." Or her mother would shout, "Cindy, hurry! You'll be late for school. No watching television after school if you're late. That's a rule."

"I think there are too many rules at our house," Cindy told her mother one day. "What I wouldn't give for a day without rules!"

"A day without rules," Cindy's mother, Mrs. Summers, said thoughtfully. "Cindy, that may not be a bad idea."

Cindy stared at her mother. *Is this the same person who reminds me to brush my teeth, comb my hair, pick up my clothes, and do the dishes?* she wondered.

"Heavens, Mom," Cindy said, "do you mean it? I can have a day without rules?"

"Tell you what," Mrs. Summers said. "We'll try it. Today there'll be no rules at our house. Everyone can do as he or she pleases."

Cindy jumped and clapped her hands.

"Great! You won't yell at me today either?" Cindy asked.

Mrs. Summers nodded. "No yelling today," she answered.

"How about making my bed?" Cindy asked. "And brushing my teeth? And cleaning my room? Do I have to do those things?"

"Only if you feel like it," Mrs. Summers answered, smiling.

Cindy did not feel like it. She ran to her room to play. It was Saturday and Cindy was excited. A whole Saturday without rules! *What fun I'll have!* she thought.

Cindy opened her closet. *What should I do first?* she wondered. It was a toss-up between paper dolls or puzzles.

Cindy decided on paper dolls. She had a brand-new paper doll book her mother bought the last time they went grocery shopping. Cindy had not even torn all the dolls out of the book yet. Carefully she punched out some of the dolls and their paper clothes from the book. She had played for only a few minutes when she heard a ripping sound behind her. She jerked her head around. "Get out of here!" Cindy shouted to her three-year-old sister, Anne.

Anne smiled and held up the paper doll she had ripped from the book. The doll's arm was missing. "Look! Me got doll too!" Anne exclaimed.

"Mo-o-o-o-ther!" Cindy yelled.

Mrs. Summers walked in the room smiling. "What is it, Cindy?" she asked softly.

"Spank her hands quick!" Cindy shouted. "Look at my poor doll!"

Mrs. Summers looked at the paper doll. She suggested Cindy get some tape to fix it.

"But spank her hands! Tell her she's not supposed to be in my things!" Cindy said.

"Remember, there are no rules at our house today," Mrs. Summers reminded Cindy. "I can't spank Anne's hands. Just tape the doll's arm, unless, of course, you don't want to." Mrs. Summers went back to the kitchen.

After Cindy taped the doll, she decided to do something else. She put the paper dolls on a high shelf where Anne could not reach them.

"Want dolls!" Anne wailed.

"If you hush up, I'll get you another toy," Cindy said. She got Anne's favorite toy, a big doll with soft, flannel pajamas. "Here, take your baby. It's crying," Cindy said.

Anne grabbed the doll and said, "Oh, nice baby, shhhhh." She rocked the doll in her little red rocking chair.

Cindy sighed with relief. She decided to watch television. Her parents only let her watch an hour of television a day. That was a rule. But since there were no rules today, Cindy flipped on some cartoons. She could watch all day if she wanted. *What fun I'll have!* Cindy thought.

No sooner had Cindy turned on the television than Anne raced into the living room with her doll and rocking chair and plopped beside Cindy. "Cartoons! My favorite!" Anne squealed with delight.

"Shhh," Cindy told her sister.

Anne started rocking her baby doll and singing, "On top of old smoky, all covered with snow . . ." as she watched cartoons.

"Shhh," Cindy said again. "I'm trying to listen."

"Me want to sing!" Anne exclaimed.

"Go to your room then," Cindy said.

Anne shook her head. "Uh-uh," she said, "me want to sing and watch TV too!"

Anne leaned back in the rocking chair and, at the top of her voice, started singing again, "On top of old smoky. . . ."

"Mo-o-o-o-ther!" Cindy shouted.

Mrs. Summers walked into the room smiling. "Yes, Cindy, what is it?"

"I can't hear the television," Cindy complained.

"That's only because your sister is singing so loud," Mrs. Summer said, still smiling. "Can't you hear her?"

"Of course I hear her!" Cindy yelled. "Can't you tell her to be quiet? I want to hear the TV."

"Sorry, I can't. No rules and yelling. Remember?"

Cindy sighed. Mrs. Summers walked out of the room.

"On top of old smoky, all covered . . ." Anne kept singing.

Cindy turned up the television, but Anne sang louder. Finally she couldn't stand it any longer. "Would you tone it down, loudmouth?" Cindy shouted.

"I know," Anne said, smiling. "Me sing song Cindy like too."

Anne started singing, "London bridge is falling down, falling down. . . ."

"I hate that song," Cindy said, turning off the television. Anne announced she had four more verses to sing. That was when Cindy decided to find something else to do. She decided a snack would taste good. "Mom, make me a snack, will you?" Cindy asked, bouncing into the living room.

Mrs. Summers was stretched on the sofa reading. "Sorry, I just don't feel like it," she said. "Guess you'll have to make your own."

"But what can I eat?" Cindy asked.

"Anything you want. No rules. Remember?"

"But I can't think of what I want," Cindy said. "Don't you have any suggestions?"

Mrs. Summers yawned. "Sorry, I just don't feel like making suggestions. I just want to read and relax."

Cindy went to the kitchen. When she opened the refrigerator, Anne was by her side. "What are you getting?" Anne asked.

Cindy slammed the refrigerator shut. "Never mind, nothing," Cindy answered. Cindy knew what she could do. She could sew a dress for her Barbie doll.

She got her yellow sewing box from the closet shelf. Her mother never let her get it out when Anne was not sleeping. That was a rule. But today Cindy could sew whenever she wanted. *What fun I'll have!* she thought.

She curled herself on a large pillow in the corner of her room. But when she started sewing, Anne grabbed the pin box and spilled all the pins on the floor.

"Mo-o-o-o-ther!" Cindy called.

This time Mrs. Summers did not even come to the room. "Don't bother me now. I'm reading," she called to Cindy.

101

"Oh, dear!" Cindy gasped as she started picking up the pins. After she had picked them all up, Cindy put the sewing box away. She would wait until Anne's nap to sew. Then Cindy remembered, no rules.

"Mother, does Anne have to take a nap today?" Cindy called.

"Only if she wants to," Cindy's mother called back.

"Oh, brotherhood!" Cindy exclaimed. Anne never wanted a nap, even when they had rules. Cindy knew she could erase the sewing project for the day. She went into the living room. "Mom, can you fix lunch now?" she asked. "I'm getting hungry."

"No, Cindy dear. No rules, remember? I don't feel like fixing lunch now. Maybe later," Mrs. Summers said.

Just then there was a loud crash. "What's that?" Cindy asked.

Mrs. Summers shrugged her shoulders. "Who cares? No rules, remember?"

Cindy groaned and ran to her room. "Oh, no!" she shouted. "Anne just broke my china teapot. *Now* will you come and spank her hands?"

Mrs. Summers walked into the room. "But, Cindy, you were the one that didn't want rules today," she said.

"Well, can't we have rules just for Anne?" Cindy asked. "She needs them!"

"That's not fair."

"But that was my favorite teapot!"

"If we have rules for one person, we need rules for everyone," Mrs. Summers explained.

Anne started playing with Cindy's china saucers and cups. "But look!" Cindy shouted. "That little pest

102

is going to break everything I own if we don't stop her! Can't you do something?"

"Sure, I can make her mind if we have rules for everyone," Mrs. Summers said.

Cindy sighed. "Well, then let's have rules for everyone."

"You're sure?" Mrs. Summers asked.

Cindy nodded. "Yeah, now I see how important rules are. Yikes! Look at Anne now!"

Anne had climbed on a chair, picked up Cindy's Bible, and was tossing it like a ball. Mrs. Summers took the Bible and gave it to Cindy. "No! No!" Mrs. Summers told Anne as she slapped Anne's hands. "That's Cindy's. You'll tear it." Even though Anne wailed, Mrs. Summers made her sit in the red rocking chair in a corner for five minutes.

While Anne was sitting in the chair, Cindy sat on the bed and opened the Bible. She had been given the Bible when she changed Sunday school grades last year, but she had not read a lot in it yet. Cindy flipped some pages.

Mrs. Summers sat beside Cindy. "I see you're looking at God's rules," Mrs. Summers said.

"Huh?" Cindy asked.

"The Bible," Mrs. Summers explained. "It tells God's rules, how he wants us to live."

Cindy gazed at the Bible. "Boy, Mom, looks like God has as many rules for us as you do for me."

"Yes," Mrs. Summers agreed, laughing. "And they're for our own good too, just like my rules are for your good. Speaking of rules, I'd better start lunch. Bet you're hungry. Then, after the dishes, I'll glue the teapot for you."

Mrs. Summers went to Anne and scooped Anne in her arms.

"Going to be good girl now and not get in Cindy's things?" Mrs. Summers asked.

"Me not get in Cindy's things," Anne said, shaking her head.

Mrs. Summers kissed Anne's cheek and the two of them trailed to the kitchen. Cindy was happy. After the dishes, she knew her mom would make Anne take a nap. That was a rule. Then Cindy could sew the dress for her Barbie doll.

> Children, it is your Christian duty to obey your parents always, for that is what pleases God.
>
> Colossians 3:20 TEV

Oh, Lord, teach me to obey my parents even when I don't feel like it. Those are the hardest times of all. Lord, help me.

A Special Heirloom

"You've got to ask your parents for a bigger allowance," Judy told Sharon.

"But I just got a 50-cent a week raise," Sharon said. "Won't that be enough?"

Judy and Sharon were making plans to buy a record album together. Judy punched more numbers on the calculator as she shook her head.

"OK. According to my calculations, you get $2.75 a week, right?" Judy asked.

"Right," Sharon answered.

"That's not enough," Judy said.

"Why not?"

Judy shook her head of short, dark hair again. "What do you mean, why not? You'll never get anywhere with $2.75 a week. Haven't your parents heard of inflation? And, on top of that, it's only two more days until Christmas. Do you know how much allowance I get?"

"Of course I don't know," Sharon said. "We've only been best friends for two days. Tell me, how much do you get?"

"Twenty dollars."

"You mean a month?" Sharon asked.

Judy put her hands on her hips, smiled, and shook her head. "I mean every week my parents give me twenty dollars allowance."

"You're rich!" Sharon exclaimed. "Is that how you got this layout?"

Judy's room was full of nice things. Her closet was stuffed with paper dolls, puzzles, games, and china tea sets. A nice assortment of blue jeans, sweaters, blouses, and socks were in the dresser drawers. Shiny books filled the bookcase. Several large stuffed animals in bright colors sat on the dresser. There was a Snoopy telephone on a yellow stand beside the bed. Attached to the stereo was a color television.

"That's not how I got *all* this stuff," Judy answered. "Some of the things, like the television and the stereo, I got for Christmas. Don't you get presents for Christmas?"

"Sure," Sharon said, smiling, "I got a real nice doll last year."

"But don't you ever get anything big?" Judy asked.

"Sure," Sharon answered. "I got Fluffo last year. That's my kitten."

"Do you have to take care of it?" Judy wanted to know.

"Sure," Sharon said. "Every day I feed it some milk and cat food."

Judy was not impressed. "I don't want anything I

have to take care of," she said, raising her hands in the air.

"But you take care of your room, don't you?" Sharon asked.

"My room?" Judy asked, frowning.

"Yeah, you know," Sharon said. "Make your bed, sweep the floor, dust your dresser. Things like that."

"The maid does that," Judy said.

"*Maid!*" Sharon exclaimed. "You've got a maid?"

"No big deal," Judy said.

"No big deal?" Sharon asked. "I've never known anyone before that had a maid."

"You're kidding!" Judy said.

"No, I'm not kidding. Your parents must be rich!" Sharon said.

"Maybe," Judy answered. "My father's a doctor and my mother is a guidance counselor at school. What do your parents do?"

"My father collects garbage," Sharon answered, smiling.

"What for? What does he do with it?" Judy wanted to know.

"He hauls it away in a big truck to the dump. I've gone with him a couple times. It's fun."

"How about your mother? What does she do?" Judy asked.

"Nothing. She stays home," Sharon answered.

Judy raised her eyebrows. "You mean, when you get home from school your mother is there waiting for you?"

Sharon nodded.

Judy was impressed. "Wow! That sounds like what you see in the movies," Judy said. "I thought everyone's mother worked."

"Nope. Not mine," Sharon answered. "Want to come over to my house tomorrow and meet her? Then you could see my room."

"Sure," Judy said. "I've never seen a mother that stays home all day and a room that a maid doesn't clean."

The next day, when Judy walked into Sharon's room, she was surprised. The room smelled clean, not like garbage. And coming from the kitchen was the most wonderful spicy aroma. Judy knew why when she saw Sharon's mother, Mrs. Wessel. Mrs. Wessel carried a tray with two big cinnamon rolls dripping with white icing.

"Want a snack, girls?" Mrs. Wessel asked. She turned to Judy and smiled. "I'm glad you could come to our house today, Judy."

"So am I," Judy said, staring at the rolls.

"Um. These are good," Judy said, after she took one of the rolls and started eating it. "What bakery store do you shop at, Mrs. Wessel?"

Sharon's mother laughed. "Thank you, Judy. I made them myself."

Judy turned to Sharon. "Thought you said your mom didn't do anything. This has got to be the best cinnamon roll I ever ate!"

After Judy and Sharon ate the rolls, they curled up on Sharon's bed and read some books. "I love this book," Judy said, holding up a green book with a torn cover. "Where can I buy one like it?"

"You can't," Sharon said. "That used to be my great-grandmother's book. My mom said they aren't even printing that book anymore."

"But the stories in it are so good. I want to read them again," Judy said.

108

"I know. That's why my grandmother gave it to me. Her mother gave the book to her when she was little," Sharon said.

"I know. I'll buy the book from you," Judy said. "How much do you want for it? I get my allowance tomorrow."

"I'd never *sell* it—it's a family heirloom!" Sharon said.

"A what?" Judy asked.

"An heirloom," Sharon said. "You know, something that has been in my family for generations. You can't buy heirlooms."

Judy sighed. Everything she had was new. Her family did not have any heirlooms. . . .

When Judy's grandmother came to visit for the Christmas holidays, Judy rushed to meet her. She always did that, and she always asked what her grandmother brought. Mrs. Donaldson always carried a sack with something in it for Judy.

"Hi, Grandmom," Judy yelled, running down the driveway. "How are you?"

The gray-haired lady smiled and gave Judy a hug. Judy took her grandmother's hand and led her inside. "Missed you, Grandmom. I've got a new friend now, Sharon, and you've got to meet her."

"I'd like that, Judy," Grandmom said. "But aren't you going to ask what I brought for you today?"

Judy looked at her grandmother's brown eyes. "Funny, but it doesn't seem so important today," she said. "Seeing you seems more important."

Mrs. Donaldson bent down and gave Judy another hug. "What more could a grandmother ask for!" she said. "And, to tell the truth, I didn't have time to do any shopping for you this time. I've been in the hospital."

Judy's eyes widened. "What for?"

Mrs. Donaldson threw her hands in the air. "Oh, nothing serious," she said. "I just fell and hurt my hip, but I'm fine now. Tomorrow, first thing in the morning, I thought we'd go Christmas shopping. You always like that."

"Grandmom, about Christmas . . ." Judy hesitated.

"Yes?" Judy's grandmother asked, raising her eyebrows.

"Well, I've been thinking," Judy said. "This year could I have something different?"

"Why, of course!" Mrs. Donaldson smiled. "We'll go into all the stores, and you can even pick out what you want. You always like to do that."

"I mean, could I have something of yours?"

"Something of mine?" Mrs. Donaldson asked, frowning.

"Yeah, you know, something you've had for a long time and don't want anymore—like an heirloom."

"Mercy!" Judy's grandmother said, smiling. "Who told you about heirlooms?"

"My friend Sharon," Judy said. "You'll like her. Her father collects garbage and her mother stays home. And Sharon's got this book that used to belong to her great-grandmother."

On Christmas Eve Judy opened a shiny blue package from her grandmother. Inside was a heart-shaped locket on a chain. Mrs. Donaldson leaned over Judy and opened the locket. Inside were two small pictures, one of a man and one of a woman.

"Who are those people?" Judy asked.

"That's your grandfather and me," Mrs. Donaldson said, smiling.

"Nice," Judy said, "I never knew grandfather."

"That's right," Mrs. Donaldson said. "He went to heaven long before you were ever born, child. But he gave me that necklace on our wedding day."

Judy gasped. "Grandmom, that means this necklace is old! It's an heirloom. Right?"

Mrs. Donaldson laughed. "That's right, my child."

Judy kissed her grandmother and asked if she could wear the necklace.

"Nothing would make me happier," Mrs. Donaldson said, still smiling.

> Command those who are rich in the things of this life . . . to place their hope, not in such an uncertain thing as riches, but in God, who generously gives us everything for our enjoyment.
>
> 1 Timothy 6:17 TEV

Bless me, Lord, with the things that count. Thank you for my parents, grandparents, friends, and teachers. As I grow up, bless me with the happiness that money cannot buy.